Dear Parent:
Your child's love of reading starts here!

Every child learns to read in a different way and at his or her own speed. You can help your young reader improve and become more confident by encouraging his or her own interests and abilities. You can also guide your child's spiritual development by reading stories with biblical values and Bible stories, like I Can Read! books published by Zonderkidz. From books your child reads with you to the first books he or she reads alone, there are I Can Read! books for every stage of reading:

SHARED READING
Basic language, word repetition, and whimsical illustrations, ideal for sharing with your emergent reader.

BEGINNING READING
Short sentences, familiar words, and simple concepts for children eager to read on their own.

READING WITH HELP
Engaging stories, longer sentences, and language play for developing readers.

READING ALONE
Complex plots, challenging vocabulary, and high-interest topics for the independent reader.

ADVANCED READING
Short paragraphs, chapters, and exciting themes for the perfect bridge to chapter books.

I Can Read! books have introduced children to the joy of reading since 1957. Featuring award-winning authors and illustrators and a fabulous cast of beloved characters, I Can Read! books set the standard for beginning readers.

A lifetime of discovery begins with the magical words **"I Can Read!"**

Visit _www.icanread.com_ for information on enriching your child's reading experience.
Visit _www.zonderkidz.com_ for more Zonderkidz I Can Read! titles.

God saw everything he had made.
And it was very good.
—*Genesis 1:31*

ZONDERKIDZ

The Beginner's Bible® God Makes the World

Copyright © 2018 by Zondervan
Illustrations © 2005, 2018 by Zondervan

Requests for information should be addressed to:
Zonderkidz, 3900 Sparks Drive SE, Grand Rapids, Michigan 49546

ISBN 978-0-310-76464-9

Illustrations: Denis Alonso

Printed in China

18 19 20 21 22 23 24 25 26 27 /DSC/ 12 11 10 9 8 7 6 5 4 3 2 1

I Can Read!™

ZONDERkidz

SHARED My First READING

The Beginner's Bible®

God Makes the World

ZONDERkidz

In the beginning,
the world was empty.
But God had a plan.

"I will make
many good things,"
God said.

On day one God said,
"I will make day and night."
So he did.

On day two God split
the water from the air.
He said, "Here are the sky
and sea."

God made land on day three.

Plants grew on the land.

Fruit trees grew there too.

On day four God put the sun
and the moon in the sky.

On day five
God made birds
to fly in the sky.

He made fish to swim
in the ocean.

Day six was busy.
God made the rest
of the animals.

Then God made the first man.

God named him Adam.

God loved Adam.

God rested on day seven.

He was so happy!

Adam was happy too.

God put Adam in a garden.

The garden was called Eden.

Adam took care of Eden.

He took care of the animals.

He even named all the animals.
"You will be called a 'parrot.'
You will be called a 'butterfly.'"

One day God made Eve.
She helped Adam take care
of the garden and the animals.

God gave Adam and Eve one rule.
God said, "Do not eat
fruit from this tree."

Later, a sneaky snake
was in the tree.

"Eve, you can eat this fruit.
It is fine!" the snake said.

Eve ate the fruit.

Then Adam ate the fruit too.

God was sad.

They had broken his one rule.

This was called "sin."

"Eve gave me the fruit,"
Adam said.

"Snake tricked me," Eve said.

God said, "Snake,
you must move on your
belly and eat dust."

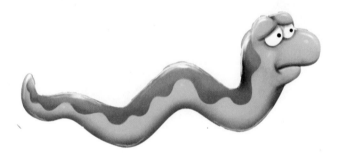

God told Adam and Eve,
"You must leave.
You did not follow my rule."

Adam and Eve left the garden.
They were very sad.

But God would always love them.

He made another plan.

One day, God would send Jesus.
Jesus would save everyone
from their sins.